★ IT'S MY STATE! ★

FLORIDA

Debra Hess

Lori P. Wiesenfeld

Marshall Cavendish
Benchmark
New York

Other Marshall Cavendish Offices:
Marshall Cavendish International (Asia) Private Limited, 1 New Industrial Road, Singapore 536196 • Marshall Cavendish International (Thailand) Co Ltd. 253 Asoke, 12th Flr, Sukhumvit 21 Road, Klongtoey Nua, Wattana, Bangkok 10110, Thailand • Marshall Cavendish (Malaysia) Sdn Bhd, Times Subang, Lot 46, Subang Hi-Tech Industrial Park, Batu Tiga, 40000 Shah Alam, Selangor Darul Ehsan, Malaysia

Marshall Cavendish is a trademark of Times Publishing Limited

All websites were available and accurate when this book was sent to press.

Library of Congress Cataloging-in-Publication Data
Hess, Debra.
    Florida / Debra Hess, Lori P. Wiesenfeld. — 2nd ed.
    p. cm. — (It's my state!)
    Includes index.
    ISBN 978-1-60870-049-3
    1. Florida—Juvenile literature. I. Wiesenfeld, Lori P. II. Title.
F311.3.H47 2011
975.9—dc22   2010003922

Second Edition developed for Marshall Cavendish Benchmark by RJF Publishing LLC (www.RJFpublishing.com)
Series Designer, Second Edition: Tammy West/Westgraphix LLC
Editor, Second Edition: Emily Dolbear

All maps, illustrations, and graphics © Marshall Cavendish Corporation. Maps and artwork on pages 6, 26, 27, 75, and back cover by Christopher Santoro. Map and graphics on pages 8 and 40 by Westgraphix LLC. Map on page 76 by Mapping Specialists.

The photographs in this book are used by permission and through the courtesy of:
Front cover: FloridianWill/Getty Images and iofoto/Shutterstock (inset).
Alamy: The Art Gallery Collection, 20; GlowImages, 22; Pat Canova, 29; Hola Images, 38, 44; Ilene McDonald, 48, 53, 54, 57; Alex Gore, 49; David R. Frazier Photolibrary, Inc, 50; Bert Hoferichter , 51; Jeff Greenberg, 59; Image Source, 62. **Florida House of Representatives:** Mark Foley, 58. **Florida State Library and Archives:** 47. **Getty Images:** Diane Macdonald, 4; Daniel J Cox, 5 (top); Rosemary Calvert, 5 (bottom); Lester Lefkowitz, 10; Sylvain Grandadam, 11; Randy Wells, 14; Stuart Westmorland, 16; Paul Sutherland, 17 (bottom); John Moran, 18 (top); Arthur Morris, 18 (bottom); James Randklev, 19; National Geographic, 24, 28; European School/The Bridgeman Art Library, 25; MPI/Stringer, 30-1, 32, 42 (top); R. B. Holt/Stringer, 34; Yale Joel/Time & Life Pictures, 36; Marilyn Angel Wynn/Nativestock.com, 41; Ray Fisher/Time & Life Pictures, 42 (bottom); Isaac Brekken/WireImage, 43; Joe Raedle, 45, 71 (top); Cindy Karp//Time & Life Pictures, 46; Simon Bruty/Sports Illustrated, 52; CULVER, WILLARD R./National Geographic, 66; Anthony-Masterson, 67; Bruce Weaver/AFP, 69; Jim Richardson/National Geographic, 72-3; Stephen Frink, 74; Bloomberg, 70; Francis Hammond, 71 (bottom). **NASA:** Jesse Allen, MODIS Rapid Response Team, NASA/GSFC, 9; Jeff Schmaltz, MODIS Rapid Response Team, NASA/GSFC, 13; GSFC, 15. **Shutterstock:** MaszaS, 60; Samot, 64; Michael Carlucci, 65. **U.S. Fish and Wildlife Service:** 17.

Printed in Malaysia (T).
135642

CONTENTS

State Tree: Sabal Palm

The majestic sabal palm, also known as sabal palmetto and cabbage palm, grows in almost any soil throughout the state of Florida. This towering tree, used for landscaping, food, and medicine, became the state tree in 1953.

State Bird: Mockingbird

Mockingbirds are usually about 10 inches (25 centimeters) long with wingspans of 15 inches (38 cm). They have grayish upper bodies, white undersides, and white patches on the tail and wings. This songbird frequently sings all night long and is a great mimic of other birds. The mockingbird became the state bird in 1927.

State Flower: Orange Blossom

Millions of these sweet-smelling white flowers bloom in central and south Florida. These flowers grow on the same tree that bears the famous Florida orange. The orange blossom was named the state flower in 1909.

State Animal: Florida Panther

This pale-brown long-tailed cat hunts white-tailed deer and other smaller animals. Since the 1700s and 1800s, many feared this cat would attack humans and farm animals. As a result, people hunted the panthers until very few remained. Destruction of the cats' natural habitat has also been a problem. The Florida panther, on the endangered species list since 1967, became the state animal in 1982.

State Reptile: American Alligator

These cold-blooded creatures like to bask in the sun on logs or riverbanks. But they move amazingly quickly over short distances. The alligator has powerful jaws and can use its swinging tail as a weapon. Fortunately, it is no longer on the endangered species list. It became the state reptile in 1987.

State Beverage: Orange Juice

Have you ever had a glass of the juice of the species *Citrus sinensis* and its hybrids? Sure you have: it is orange juice! In 1967, it became Florida's official state beverage.

The Sunshine State

More than 80 million people travel to Florida every year for its sunny beaches, refreshing water, and other attractions. But Florida is so much more than a dream vacation spot. North of the beaches lie rolling hills and lush forests, while in the south a sprawling national park is home to hundreds of different endangered plants and animals.

Landscape and Regions

Florida is the southernmost state in the continental United States (Hawaii is farther south). The largest part of Florida is a peninsula that projects about 400 miles (640 kilometers) into the sea. A peninsula is land that is surrounded by water on three sides. The northern part of Florida runs along the shore of the Gulf of Mexico. It is called the panhandle because it is shaped like the handle of a frying pan. The southern tip of the state is less than 100 miles (160 km) from Cuba.

Florida's current size and shape are a result of millions of years of geological change. Large pieces of rock, called plates, lie beneath Earth's surface. Over time these plates move around, combining and

Quick Facts

FLORIDA BORDERS

North	Georgia
	Alabama
South	Straits of Florida
East	Atlantic Ocean
West	Alabama
	Gulf of Mexico

Florida Counties

Florida has 67 counties.

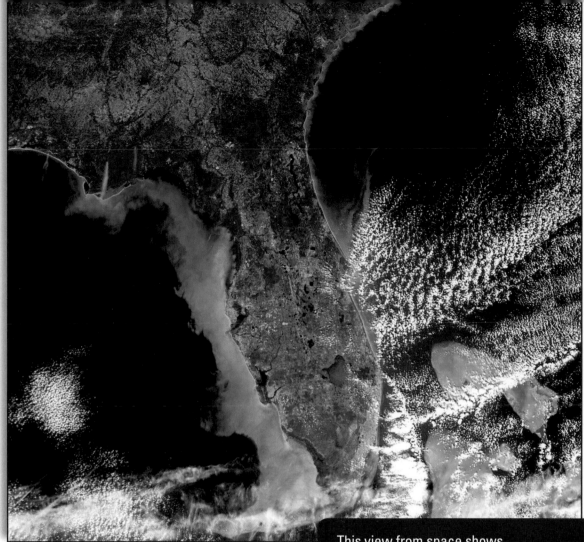

This view from space shows Florida, the Gulf of Mexico to the west, and the Atlantic Ocean to the east.

breaking landmasses, and shaping the features of Earth's surface. Erosion—the process of being worn away by wind, rain, and water current—changed Florida's shape and landscape. Dirt, sand, shells, and rocks brought by the wind and ocean currents also shaped parts of Florida. Over time, sea creatures such as coral and mollusks lived and died on the coasts of Florida. Their remains hardened into rocks and minerals and added mass to Florida's coasts.

Quick Facts

FLORIDA'S COUNTIES
Of Florida's sixty-seven counties, only one is named for an animal—manatee, the endangered mammal that lives in Florida's waters.

Florida's Coastal Lowlands are famous for their long stretches of sandy beaches.

One million years ago, Earth's climate turned much colder. Large amounts of ocean water turned into ice, and large masses of ice called glaciers covered much of the planet. As a result, the water level in the oceans sank, and at that time, the land that is now Florida was twice its current size. When this Ice Age ended, water levels rose, and much of that land was covered. The rise in water levels also formed swamps.

The Florida peninsula lies on the relatively flat land formation called the Florida Platform. The highest point in the entire state—only 345 feet (105 meters) high—is Britton Hill, in the north. Florida has 53,927 square miles (139,670 sq km) of land, making it the twenty-sixth-largest state in the country.

The area of Florida known as the Coastal Lowlands stretches around the coastal borders of the state. The lowlands are covered with forests of sabal palm and cypress. The best-known area of the Coastal Lowlands is the Everglades. The Everglades cover a large portion of the state, stretching from Lake Okeechobee, the state's largest lake, to the Gulf of Mexico. Mangrove trees, ferns, and a razor-sharp plant called saw grass cover much of this marshy wetland. The wildlife in the park includes alligators, waterfowl, and hundreds of kinds of frogs, turtles, and snakes.

For many years, people considered the Everglades a worthless swamp. Developers began to drain the

An alligator basks in the sun in the Everglades.

Everglades in order to use the land. They had dreams of building hotels and tourist resorts in this region. Wildlife was killed, and habitats were destroyed.

Since the 1930s, many nature enthusiasts, such as Ernest F. Coe, worked toward passing laws to protect the Everglades. In 1947, Marjory Stoneman Douglas wrote *The Everglades: River of Grass*, a book that called attention to the wonders of the Everglades, begging the world to preserve its fragile ecosystem. Many plants and animals living there were endangered. Destroying their habitat would make them disappear forever. The efforts of the Everglades' supporters paid off in 1947 when President Harry Truman dedicated Everglades National Park, protecting a large portion of the region—and the wildlife within it—from development.

The southernmost parts of the state are called the Florida Keys. This chain of islands is 110 miles (177 km) long. It stretches from Biscayne Bay—located on the southeastern coast of Florida—southwest, toward the Gulf of Mexico. The only living coral reef in the United States is here. Some of the islands also have tropical forests. But many people live on the islands in close-knit communities. Bridges and the Overseas Highway connect most of the islands. But some islands can be reached only by boat. Key West, on the western end of the islands, is the southernmost city in the continental United States.

Florida's highest points rise from the sea with hilly pine forests in the northwestern corner of the state. The Western Highlands are low compared to

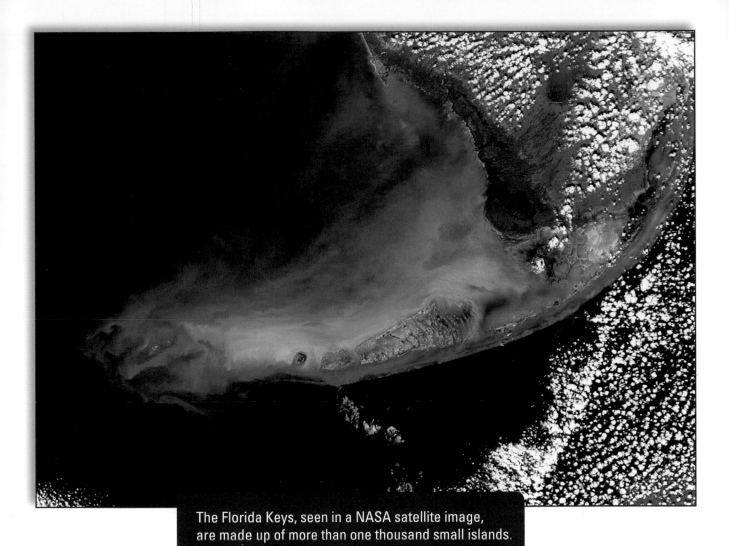

The Florida Keys, seen in a NASA satellite image, are made up of more than one thousand small islands.

many other parts of the United States. Rolling hills and small villages surround the highlands.

East of the Western Highlands and north of the Coastal Lowlands are the Marianna Lowlands. Hills and valleys make up this section of Florida, where many people still farm. The Tallahassee Hills lie farther east. Oak and pine trees cover the hills, which slope toward the famous Suwannee River to the east. The Suwannee River flows south from the Okefenokee Swamp in Georgia, down through parts of Florida, and into the Gulf of Mexico. In the center of the Florida peninsula is a 250-mile (400-km) stretch of land known as the Central Highlands. Flat grassy plains, citrus groves, and lakeside communities make up this area.

DRY TORTUGAS
Spanish explorer Juan Ponce de León discovered the Tortugas—islands at the western end of the Florida Keys, now part of Dry Tortugas National Park—in 1513. He named the islands for the many sea turtles, or *tortugas* in Spanish, that he found there. Because there was no fresh water, he called the Tortugas "dry."

The United States began building Dry Tortugas National Park's Fort Jefferson in the mid–1800s to protect its shipping channel. Work on the massive structure was never completed, however.

Climate

Florida's climate is hot and humid. Heavy rains fall from April to November. As one native Floridian said of the rain and humidity, "We may not have to deal with cold and snow, but Florida is a bad hair state."

The state has the longest coastline of any U.S. state except Alaska. When temperatures soar, there are plenty of coastal places to swim and cool off.

Floridians may not have to deal with freezing temperatures and snowstorms, but from the beginning of June to the end of November, they have to worry about hurricanes. A hurricane is a tropical storm with wind speeds of at least 74 miles per hour (119 kph). A hurricane begins over an ocean, where the sun warms the surface of the water and causes the water to evaporate. The evaporated water floats into the air and forms thunderclouds. The rotation of Earth sends these storm clouds spinning toward land. When a hurricane hits a developed area, the flooding can destroy buildings and kill people.

In this time-lapse image, Hurricane Andrew approaches the Florida coast from the east and moves on to the Gulf of Mexico.

More hurricanes strike Florida than any other state. The damage can be massive. In 1992, Hurricane Andrew caused sixty-five deaths and destruction that totaled $25 billion. But Floridians worked together with people from other parts of the country to repair and rebuild their communities.

Wildlife

More than ninety species of mammals live in different parts of the state, including the black bear, puma, gray fox, and otter. More types of fish and shellfish are found in Florida's waters than in any other part of the world. The coastal waters are filled with shrimp, oysters, crabs, scallops, clams, conchs, and crayfish. Bass and catfish swim in the freshwater lakes and rivers. The oceans are full of grouper,

Bottlenose dolphins, found in warm waters around the world, can weigh more than 600 pounds (270 kilograms).

mackerel, marlin, and trout. More than one thousand species of fish have been identified in Florida's waters.

Fish are not the only animals you will find in the water. Bottlenose dolphins inhabit Florida's coastal waters. But swimming with or feeding dolphins can be dangerous for both humans and animals. When traveling through the swamp, animals—including humans—must look out for alligators lurking in the waters.

Five hundred species of wild birds soar over Florida's waters and land. These include quail, cuckoos, ospreys, pelicans, woodpeckers, robins, pigeons, storks, and bald eagles. On the water you might see herons, ducks, ibis, egrets, or flamingos. Wild turkeys also roam across some of Florida's woodlands and open forests. Human activity and the resulting changes to the environment almost completely killed off some of these birds. The bald eagle, a well-known symbol of the United States, thrives in the state, under a careful state management plan, after being removed from the federal threatened species list in 1997. (If an animal or plant is threatened, that means it is likely to become endangered.) The flamingo, heron, egret, and ibis almost became extinct in the 1800s after hunters killed them for their feathers, which were sold to hatmakers. Today, places such as Everglades National Park protect these beautiful birds.

The wood stork and Florida manatee are examples of the state's endangered animals. Endangered animals once had large populations, but now only very few animals remain. Their numbers decreased when hunters killed them for skins, feathers, or food. Car accidents (or collisions with boats in the case of the manatee) and habitat destruction also reduced their populations. The federal government stepped in and listed these animals as endangered species.

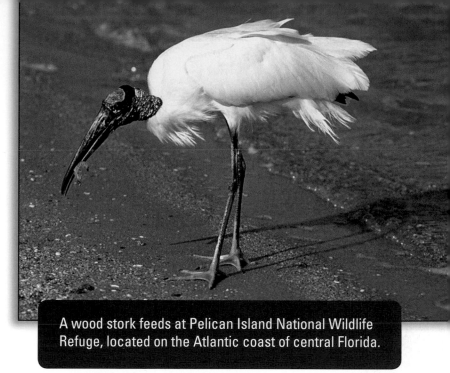

A wood stork feeds at Pelican Island National Wildlife Refuge, located on the Atlantic coast of central Florida.

Once an animal is listed as endangered, it is illegal to hunt that animal or harm it in any way. Some endangered animals are taken to protected places. Sometimes humans try to recreate the animals' natural habitat to help them live longer and breed. The Everglades is home to many endangered animals. Through the efforts of Floridians and nature lovers across the country, many endangered animals and plants have had a chance to increase their numbers and survive.

The manatee, a slow-moving mammal that eats plants, is sometimes called a sea cow.

Plants & Animals

Flamingo

Flamingos can sometimes be found in the marshy wetlands of the Everglades or in the waters along the Keys. The flamingo population in the state, however, has decreased as a result of land development, pollution, and other environmental changes.

Sea Turtles

Five types of sea turtles live in Florida's waters. Green, hawksbill, Kemp's ridley, and leatherback turtles are endangered, and the loggerhead is threatened, or likely to become endangered.

Marsh Rabbit

These brown rabbits live in the state's freshwater and saltwater marshes and swamps. They are nocturnal, which means they come out at night, and feed on the marsh plants. Marsh rabbits make their homes on land, but if they need to, they can get into the water and swim. A subspecies, the Lower Keys marsh rabbit, is endangered.

Cypress

The bald cypress, which grows into a giant tree, is normally found by lakes, in swamps, and along streams. The pond cypress tree, a much smaller variety, grows in ponds with still or slow-moving water. It is native to the Everglades.

Southern Magnolia

The southern magnolia, also known as the evergreen magnolia, grows anywhere from 60 to 90 feet (18 to 28 m) in height. The magnolias have bright green leaves and large white fragrant flowers. The trees are usually planted for their beauty rather than for use.

Florida Manatee

The manatee is a large, gentle marine mammal that lives in Florida's warm waters. Each year, many manatees are injured or killed by boats, by getting tangled in fishing lines, or by eating litter or fishing hooks. Land development has also decreased the manatees' natural habitat. The Florida manatee is an endangered species.

From the Beginning

The history of Florida is one of many people from different nations seeking a better life in a land they saw as golden. Florida is sometimes called "the state where everybody is from somewhere else." But all these people—native and new—are an important part of the state's history.

The First Floridians

No one really knows when the first humans arrived in today's Florida. But many experts think that American Indians first reached the peninsula about 12,000 years ago. They believe that some of them might have come from present-day Central and South America, crossing the water into what is now the southern part of the state. Other American Indians might have come from the northwestern part of today's United States. These natives might have walked across the icy land bridge that used to exist between Asia and North America.

Some large, dirt-covered mounds built by early American Indians exist in the state today. They are called burial mounds. In many cases, the mounds contain human remains, religious artifacts, pottery, and jewelry.

It is estimated that when Europeans first arrived in the early sixteenth century, more than 100,000 American Indians lived in present-day Florida. The Calusa and Tequesta tribes lived in the south. These natives were hunters and gatherers. They speared fish for food, and they hunted bears, deer, and alligators

American Indians lived in today's Florida before the Europeans arrived in the early sixteenth century. In this sixteenth-century engraving, Timucua Indians paddle in a canoe by their stored grain.

with bows and arrows and clubs. They killed these animals for food and for clothing. The Timucua people, who lived in today's central and northeastern part of the state, hunted animals and maintained farms. The Apalachee people, who lived in the northwest, were also hunters and farmers. Both groups farmed corn, beans, squash, and pumpkins.

The Europeans Arrive

The written history of Florida begins in 1513 with a search for the fountain of youth. Some people believed that drinking from this fountain could keep a person young. King Ferdinand of Spain sent an explorer named Juan Ponce de León in search of this fountain in a land called Bimini. But Bimini did not exist. Instead, Ponce de León and his men landed on the northeast coast of what is now Florida. It was on the day of *Pascua Florida* (Feast of the Flowers), which is Spain's Eastertime celebration. The explorer named the land *la Florida* in honor of the feast.

Ponce de León explored la Florida and its surroundings before sailing to Puerto Rico. In 1521, the explorer

This statue of Spanish explorer Ponce de León can be found in Saint Augustine.

returned with two hundred people, fifty horses, and many supplies. His idea was to colonize the land for Spain. But fights with American Indians made this too difficult. Ponce de León was wounded in one of these fights and sailed to Cuba, where he died.

Despite this setback, explorers continued to come to the region. In 1539, another Spanish explorer, Hernando de Soto, journeyed to the area in search of silver and gold, landing along the shore of what is now called Tampa Bay. But no great treasure awaited Hernando de Soto and his men. After exploring the southeast for several years, de Soto died from a fever in 1542 in present-day Louisiana, and the rest of his expedition went to Mexico. In 1559, Tristán de Luna y Arellano led another Spanish expedition to colonize today's Florida. He established a settlement at Pensacola Bay, but it was abandoned within two years after a series of misfortunes including illness and lack of food.

Besides searching for treasure, new trade routes, and land to colonize, many Europeans came to the area to spread the Catholic religion. Priests came hoping to convert the natives. The American Indians had their own religions, which were very different from Christianity. Many did not want to convert. They were often beaten or killed when they refused. Other natives willingly converted. Still others, afraid and overpowered by the Europeans, practiced Christianity because they had no other choice.

During this time, many Spanish ships filled with treasures sailed the seas off the coast of present-day Florida. Most of them were headed back to Spain. The ships could carry a crew of about two hundred men. The chests of gold and silver were kept under guard in a room on the lower deck of the ship. But before they could reach Europe, many of these ships sank to the bottom of the ocean. Divers have found remains of some sunken treasure ships, while other vessels remain lost in the waters off Florida.

> **Quick Facts**
>
> **HERNANDO DE SOTO**
> In 1539, Hernando de Soto brought the first pigs to what is now Florida, as food for his men. Many of the pigs escaped, and their descendants still live in the wild in Florida today.

The Spanish were not the only Europeans interested in colonizing Florida. The French began explorations, trying to claim Florida for France. A French explorer named Jean Ribault traveled through the area in 1562. By 1564, the French had established Fort Caroline along the Saint Johns River, near present-day Jacksonville.

Spain did not want the French to gain control over Florida. Pedro Menéndez de Avilés was sent to Florida to remove the French and strengthen Spanish control over the land. In 1565, he established a settlement on the Atlantic coast called San Agustín (Saint Augustine). It was the first permanent European

The Spanish, led by Pedro Menéndez de Avilés, dedicated San Agustín (Saint Augustine) in 1565.

This map illustrates the 1586 destruction of Saint Augustine by the English fleet commanded by Sir Francis Drake.

settlement in what would later become the United States. Menéndez de Avilés and his men killed most of the French settlers. They took Fort Caroline from the French and renamed it San Mateo.

The French fought back two years later, when Dominique de Gourgues recaptured San Mateo and executed the Spanish soldiers stationed there. But the Spanish continued to set up forts and Catholic missions all across the region of northern Florida.

The English were also interested in controlling Florida. In 1586, the English captain Sir Francis Drake looted and burned Saint Augustine, although Spain still controlled Florida and most of what is now the southeastern section of the United States. But the English wanted more land and gradually captured it from the Spanish.

MAKING A MEDALLION

Jewelry, medallions, and other ornaments were often part of a wrecked ship's treasure. With the help of an adult, you can make your own medallion. The medallion will have a compass rose—the symbol used on maps to show north, east, and other directions.

WHAT YOU NEED

Oven

Newspapers

Aluminum foil

Two or more colors of clay that can be baked in your kitchen oven—totaling about $\frac{1}{2}$ block

Metal jar lid

Old table knife

Nail

Pot holder

Cooling rack

2 feet (60 cm) of yarn

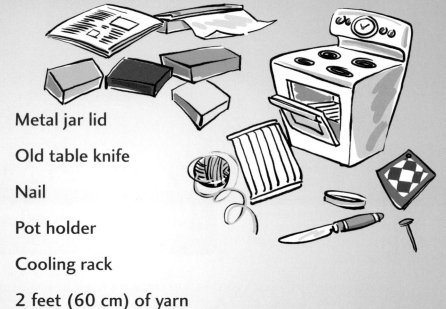

Preheat the oven according to the directions on the clay's package. Please ask an adult to help you with the oven.

Cover your work surface with a large piece of newspaper, then a piece of aluminum foil.

Using different colors, make four balls of clay, each in a different size. The balls can range in size from as small as possible to about the size of a golf ball. Flatten the balls into circles with the back of the lid. Try to make the circles very thin.

Choose the largest as your base and set it aside. Also set aside the smallest circle. With the knife, cut the other two circles into eight equal wedges like pie slices. Carefully separate the wedges.

Arrange four wedges from the larger circle evenly on your base, with the tips pointing out. Leave space in the middle. (On a compass rose, these wedges represent north, east, south, and west.) Arrange four more wedges from the other circle between them. These wedges should also point outward, representing northeast, southeast, southwest, and northwest. Place the smallest flattened circle on top of all of the wedges.

Use the nail to make a hole near the top of the base large enough to slide a piece of yarn through. Make sure to leave 1/4 inch (about 5 millimeters) between the edge of the base and the hole.

Have an adult pick up the foil with the medallion on it and place both in the oven. Bake according to the directions included with the clay.

Then ask an adult to help you remove the medallion from the oven—it might be very hot! Place the foil and medallion on a cooling rack. When the medallion is completely cool, thread the yarn through the hole and tie the ends of the yarn together into a knot. You can wear your medallion or just display it, imagining that you have discovered sunken treasure.

Conflict and Changing Control

In 1702, English colonists in the Carolinas attacked Spanish Florida and again destroyed the town of Saint Augustine. But the Spanish fort there—Castillo de San Marcos—remained under Spain's control. The English colonists continued to take Spanish lands from Tallahassee to Saint Augustine. They destroyed Spanish missions and killed or took as slaves many American Indians. The French, from their colony in Louisiana, pushed against Spanish Florida's western border and captured Pensacola in 1719, twenty-one years after the town had been established. After years of attacks from the British and French, Spain's power in the region had weakened. The British continued to move southward. By 1733, Georgia, which bordered Spanish Florida, was the southernmost British colony. Colonists living in Georgia continued to extend the colony's borders and fight the Spanish in Florida.

During the mid–1700s, Britain and France fought each other in North America in a conflict called the French and Indian War. Spain sided with the

Spanish soldiers at Castillo de San Marcos, their fort in Saint Augustine, fire cannons to repel a British attack.

French during some of the fighting. When the war ended with a British victory in 1763, France lost almost all its land in eastern North America. The British took control of this land. During the war, the British had captured Havana on the island of Cuba, which had been controlled by Spain. Spain traded Florida to Britain in order to get back Havana. The British now controlled Florida.

Britain split Florida into two colonies. East Florida's capital was Saint Augustine, and Pensacola was the capital of West Florida. British control of the two Floridas lasted until Spanish troops marched back into West Florida during the American Revolution, which lasted from 1775 to 1783. The British surrendered parts of Florida to Spain in 1781. After they lost the war, the British gave up all of Florida to Spain. In 1783, Spain was once again in control of Florida.

But the end of the American Revolution was not an end to war in the region. Much of Florida still saw fighting. After the Revolution, Britain continued to encourage American Indians, including the Seminoles and Creeks, to fight against American settlers. The British provided the natives with supplies and weapons to aid in these fights. The War of 1812, a result of unresolved problems between the United States and Britain, also brought unrest to the area.

Some Americans in the Southern states, whose economies depended on African-American slave labor, were not pleased with Spanish control of Florida because slaves could flee across the border

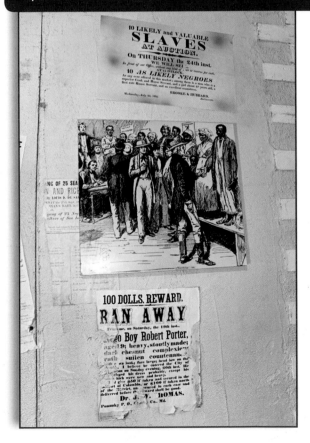

These historical posters on display at Gainesville's Florida Museum of Natural History advertise slave auctions (top) and offer a reward for a young escaped slave (bottom). Before Florida became part of the United States, some slaves escaped to freedom in the Spanish-controlled land.

to freedom there. Many of these escaped slaves joined with the Seminoles. Americans in Georgia especially, as well as the federal government, were interested in making Florida part of the United States. Spanish control over Florida was weak, so U.S. troops continued to push into Florida, engaging in fighting against American Indians and African Americans there. This fighting escalated into the First Seminole War (1817–1818). During this war, U.S. general Andrew Jackson commanded the troops that fought the Seminoles and African Americans and captured major Spanish settlements. Under an 1819 treaty, Spain agreed to give Florida to the United States. It officially became part of the United States in 1821, and Andrew Jackson served as the territorial governor for a few months.

From Territory to State

After Florida became a territory, the two Floridas were combined, with Tallahassee as the new capital. Established in 1824, the city was chosen because it was halfway between the former capitals of Saint Augustine and Pensacola.

But peace did not come to Florida. As more and more people moved to the new territory, the white settlers decided they wanted American Indian land. They also wanted escaped slaves removed from their Florida lands. In 1835, the Second Seminole War broke out between the U.S. government and the Seminole people, who did not want to leave their homeland and relocate west of the Mississippi River. By that time, Andrew Jackson was the president of the United States. The war ended in 1842, and the Seminoles were forced off their land. Some Seminoles left voluntarily, and some were

The Second Seminole War broke out in 1835 when the Seminole people resisted the U.S. government's attempt to relocate them.

captured and sent to reservations in the West. But others escaped and made new lives in Florida's Everglades.

In 1845, Florida became the twenty-seventh state. By 1850, the state's population had reached 87,445. In 1855, Florida's legislature passed the Internal Improvement Act. Public land was offered to people who wanted to build businesses in Florida. Some transportation-industry businesses moved to Florida because of this act. The Third Seminole War (1855–1858) resulted in the forced relocation of more Seminoles to the West.

The Civil War

From the time the British first established colonies in North America, Southern plantation owners relied on African-American slaves to work their fields. To many white Southerners, this was their way of life. Without slaves, crops could

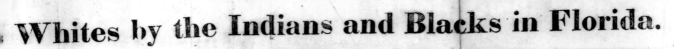

orrid Massacre of the Whites in Florida, in December 1835, and January, February, March and April 1836, when ndred (including women and children) fell victims to the barbarity of the Negroes and Indians.

Confederate soldiers, wearing assorted uniforms, pose for a photograph in 1861 at Pensacola's Warrington Navy Yard.

not be grown, sold, or traded, and white landowners in the South would suffer. Florida had many of these plantations.

The Northern way of life was different. The North's economy did not depend on large plantations. Some antislavery states in the North thought that the slave states in the South were too powerful. Many Northerners also felt that slavery was morally wrong. These two issues helped lead to the Civil War.

Most Florida voters were not against slavery. When Abraham Lincoln ran for president in 1860, many Floridians disagreed with his politics, especially his antislavery position. Lincoln won the election. On January 10, 1861, Florida seceded, or withdrew, from the Union (another name for the United States at the time). Florida was one of the eleven states that left the Union and joined together to form the Confederate States of America, leading to the Civil War.

Though very few Civil War battles were fought on Florida soil, Union forces occupied many of the coastal towns and forts. The interior of the state remained in Confederate hands, however.

Florida provided about 15,000 troops to the Confederate war effort, although more than 2,000 Floridians fought for the North. The state also provided many supplies, including salt, beef, pork, and cotton, to the Confederate army. In the end, the South was defeated, and Union troops took over the capital city of Tallahassee on May 10, 1865. Florida was once again part of the United States, though it was not officially readmitted to the Union as a state until 1868.

Rebuilding and Growth

After so many years of fighting, Florida and other Southern states were in bad shape. The war had damaged their economies, and relations between Southerners and Northerners were poor. African Americans in the state still faced many problems. Many white people did not want to treat black people equally. After the Civil War, the federal government passed laws to protect the rights of black people. At the end of 1865, the Thirteenth Amendment to the U.S. Constitution, abolishing slavery in the United States, was ratified. With help from the federal government, Southern states set up new state governments, rejoined the Union, and began to restore their economies. Slowly, the Southern states were rebuilt.

During the late nineteenth century, Florida's economy grew stronger. Cattle raising became an important industry, as did growing citrus fruits such as oranges, grapefruits, and lemons. The Florida orange was becoming famous. The growth of these industries throughout the state prompted the construction of many roads and railroads.

By the early 1900s, Florida's population and wealth were increasing. The invention and popularity of automobiles made it even easier for people to travel to Florida. Many stayed on and contributed to the state's growth. But the good times did not last.

Hard Times and Wars

World War I lasted from 1914 to 1918. In 1917, the United States entered the war, joining several other countries—including France, Great Britain, Russia, and Italy—to fight against Germany, Austria-Hungary, Turkey, and Bulgaria. Florida provided supplies to the war effort. Many Floridians served in the military at this time. Some were sent overseas to fight in Europe.

The 1920s were difficult for Florida. Powerful hurricanes hit the state in 1926 and 1928. These storms killed so many fruit trees and destroyed so many

The Miami area was devastated by the 1926 hurricane, which damaged fruit trees, homes, and businesses. The devastation marked the end of the Florida land boom.

homes and businesses that Florida's economy was badly hurt. Then, in 1929, Mediterranean fruit flies invaded many parts of the state, destroying crops. The citrus business was hit hard. Army troops set up roadblocks to stop people from bringing more infected fruit into the state. Florida's citrus production was reduced by more than half.

That same year, the entire country saw the beginning of what came to be called the Great Depression. Banks closed, and many businesses failed. Workers lost their jobs, and many families did not have enough money for food. People stopped traveling, and Florida's railroad companies were hurt. Florida was already experiencing hard times. The Great Depression, which lasted for about ten years, made the situation even worse.

After Japanese warplanes bombed the U.S. naval base at Pearl Harbor, Hawaii, in 1941, the United States entered World War II, joining the fighting against the governments of Germany, Japan, and Italy. World War II, which had begun in Europe in 1939, lasted until 1945. Once again, Florida provided necessary supplies for the troops. As in World War I, Floridians served in the military. Because of its warm climate, Florida became a major training center for U.S. soldiers, sailors, and pilots. More highways and airports were built to accommodate the increased traffic. These roads and airports became useful after the war, helping Florida's economy to grow.

Growth and Prosperity

Florida has experienced enormous population growth since World War II. Once one of the least populated and developed states in the nation, Florida became, by the early twenty-first century, the South's most populous state and the fourth most populous in the country. The growth occurred because Florida had a desirable climate and inexpensive land. The southern state was seen as a welcoming place.

Throughout the state's history, tourism has always played an important role. But in the last part of the twentieth century, Florida tourism boomed. Thanks in large part to the opening of Walt Disney World, near Orlando, in 1971, Florida

Disney characters and park staff gather in front of Cinderella's Castle, shortly before the opening of Walt Disney World in 1971.

became the family vacation hot spot of the world. Visitors came for the theme parks as well as Florida's sunny beaches. Tourists wanted to see unique natural sites such as the Everglades and the Florida Keys. Through the years, many people have come to explore the islands, swim in the warm waters, see the coral reefs, and take part in the offshore fishing.

The citrus and fishing industries continued to bring money into the state. Mining and the new space and military technology industries also contributed to Florida's newfound prosperity. More businesses provided thousands of jobs.

Like other states, Florida was severely affected by the bad economic times that hit the country hard beginning in 2008. Many workers lost their jobs, some people could not afford to stay in their homes, and the tourist industry was hurt as fewer Americans had money to travel. Financial help from the federal government helped Florida's government and people cope with these problems as they looked forward to renewed economic growth and prosperity.

Important Dates

★ **1513** Spanish explorer Juan Ponce de León lands on the northeast coast of present-day Florida.

★ **1539** Hernando de Soto explores Florida in search of silver and gold.

★ **1562** Frenchman Jean Ribault explores the area.

★ **1564** The French establish Fort Caroline.

★ **1565** Spaniard Pedro Menéndez de Avilés establishes San Agustín (Saint Augustine).

★ **1763** The British gain control of Florida from Spain. The British split Florida into two parts.

★ **1783** After the American Revolution, Spain regains control of Florida.

★ **1817–1818** The First Seminole War is fought.

★ **1821** Florida becomes a U.S. territory.

★ **1835–1842** The Second Seminole War is fought, and Seminoles are forced to leave their homeland.

★ **1845** Florida becomes the twenty-seventh state.

★ **1855–1858** The Third Seminole War results in the forced relocation of more Seminoles to the West.

★ **1861** Florida secedes from the Union and joins the Confederacy. The Civil War begins.

★ **1868** Florida is readmitted to the Union as a state.

★ **1941–1945** Florida is a major training center for U.S. soldiers, sailors, and pilots during World War II.

★ **1961** NASA launches Alan B. Shepard Jr. into space from Cape Canaveral.

★ **1971** Walt Disney World opens.

★ **1986** The space shuttle *Challenger* explodes seventy-three seconds after launch from Cape Canaveral, killing all seven crew members.

★ **1992** Hurricane Andrew hits Florida and other areas in the southeastern United States.

★ **2006** The Miami Heat wins its first NBA Final.

The People

The Sunshine State is home to more than 18 million people. Florida is the fourth-most-populous state in the nation, behind California, Texas, and New York. The state's population has also grown rapidly in recent decades, as people from other states and also from other countries have moved to the Sunshine State in large numbers. Florida's population has almost doubled just since 1980. As recently as 1960, fewer than 5 million people lived in Florida.

According to 2007 U.S. Census Bureau estimates, the population of Florida was 76.3 percent white, 15.3 percent African American, and 2.2 percent Asian American. About 20 percent was Hispanic (Hispanics may be of any race). Reflecting the fact that many people from other states choose to retire in Florida, the state has the highest percentage of people age sixty-five and over. Today, Floridians share their cultures, traditions, and opinions to make Florida such a diverse state.

Native Floridians

The original American Indians of Florida, including the Timucua, Calusa, Apalachee, and Tequesta tribes, were killed by disease or warfare, were captured as slaves, or were forced to leave Florida by the Spaniards. The Seminole Indians, descendants of many American Indian tribes, had first come to Florida in the 1700s in search of new places to build homes. By the 1850s, when the

Floridians young and old enjoy warm weather year-round.

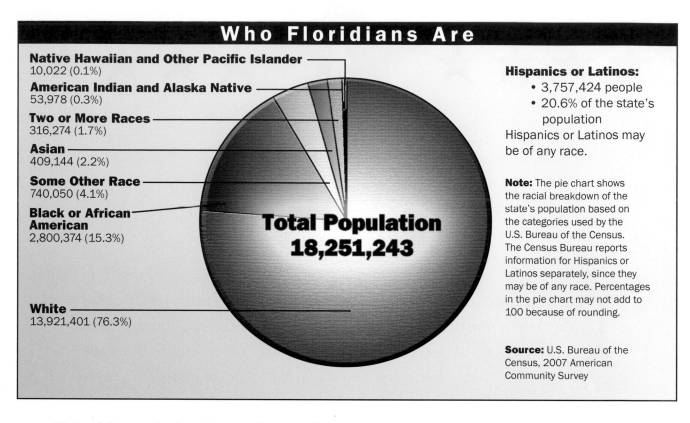

Who Floridians Are

Native Hawaiian and Other Pacific Islander
10,022 (0.1%)

American Indian and Alaska Native
53,978 (0.3%)

Two or More Races
316,274 (1.7%)

Asian
409,144 (2.2%)

Some Other Race
740,050 (4.1%)

Black or African American
2,800,374 (15.3%)

White
13,921,401 (76.3%)

Total Population 18,251,243

Hispanics or Latinos:
- 3,757,424 people
- 20.6% of the state's population

Hispanics or Latinos may be of any race.

Note: The pie chart shows the racial breakdown of the state's population based on the categories used by the U.S. Bureau of the Census. The Census Bureau reports information for Hispanics or Latinos separately, since they may be of any race. Percentages in the pie chart may not add to 100 because of rounding.

Source: U.S. Bureau of the Census, 2007 American Community Survey

United States declared an end to conflicts with the Seminoles, thousands of these natives had been moved to reservations in the western United States. Some Seminoles remained in Florida by living in the swamps where U.S. soldiers and settlers could not find them. Most of today's Seminoles are the descendants of these Indians. Today, the state has six Seminole reservations, where more than two thousand Indians live.

The Seminoles have developed a strong economy to support their way of life. Tourism is one way Seminoles earn money. The Seminoles have a cultural museum

In Their Own Words

How could there be a better place to live—we have perfect weather AND Disney World! Well, except for the hurricanes and going to school when it's too hot.

—Amanda, an eleven-year-old from Orlando

as well as other tourist attractions, such as ecotours of the Florida Everglades. Visitors come to the reservations to enjoy these sites and learn more about the Seminole culture. Tourists also visit the reservations' casinos. Many Seminoles make a successful living in the citrus and cattle industries. The money that comes from tourism and agriculture helps pay for Seminole schools and health care.

The Seminoles also try to keep their traditions alive. They design some buildings like their ancestors' palm-thatched homes called *chickees*, although they do not live in them anymore. Many Seminoles wear colorful patchwork clothing of the past. Storytelling is an important part of the culture, and the tribe's legends are passed down from old to young. The Seminoles are eager to share their history and culture with others. Some Seminoles visit schools in different parts of Florida to teach students about their traditions and their long history in the state. Seminoles also share their culture at the state's many American Indian festivals.

The Seminoles hold festivals all over Florida. This boy competes in an archery contest during a Big Cypress Indian Reservation festival.

Famous Floridians

Osceola: Seminole Leader

Osceola, born in about 1800, was a Seminole leader who led successful battles against five U.S. generals during the Second Seminole War. When Osceola and other Seminole leaders met Americans for peace negotiations in 1837, General Thomas Jesup ordered them imprisoned. People consider Osceola's capture one of the blackest marks in the country's military history. Osceola died in a South Carolina fort prison in 1838.

John Ringling: Circus Professional

John Ringling, born in 1866, and four of his brothers started the Ringling Brothers Circus in 1884. A performer early on, he later took on a management role and helped make the circus a huge success. In the 1920s, Ringling and his wife bought land in Sarasota, Florida, which became the winter home of the circus. They also built a mansion and a building to hold their art collection. This is now the John and Mable Ringling Museum of Art.

Marjory Stoneman Douglas: Writer and Activist

Marjory Stoneman Douglas, born in Minnesota in 1890, moved to Miami in 1915. A respected writer who fought for women's rights, racial equality, and environmentalism, Douglas is most famous for her dedication to preserving the Everglades. She is often called the "mother" or the "defender" of the Everglades. Douglas died in 1998 at the age of 108. Her ashes were spread throughout her beloved Everglades.

Mildred "Babe" Didrikson Zaharias: Athlete

"Babe" Didrikson Zaharias was born in Texas about 1914, but she made Florida her home. A talented athlete, Zaharias excelled at a time when most women were not even allowed to play professional sports. A pro golfer, she was also accomplished in basketball, track, baseball, tennis, swimming, diving, boxing, volleyball, handball, bowling, billiards, skating, and cycling. She won gold medals in the 1932 Olympics in the 80-meter hurdles and javelin throw.

Ray Charles: Musician

Though he was born in Georgia in 1930, Ray Charles was raised in Greenville, Florida. By the age of seven, Charles was completely blind. He learned to play the piano, saxophone, and clarinet. He also started to compose and arrange music. He played country-and-western music, jazz, soul, gospel, and blues. Charles, who died in 2004, is respected for his triumphs over poverty, disability, and racism as well as his contributions to the music world.

Enrique Iglesias: Singer/Songwriter

Enrique Iglesias was born in Spain in 1975 but moved in 1982 to Miami to live with his father, singer Julio Iglesias. Enrique's interest in music began when he was in school. His 1995 debut was a Spanish-language album that sold one million copies and won a Grammy Award. He has since released numerous albums, both in Spanish and in English, selling millions of copies worldwide.

Cuban Americans

In 2007, about 80 percent of Floridians were born in the United States. Of those born outside the United States, about 20 percent came from the neighboring island of Cuba. Since 1959, when Fidel Castro came to power and established a Communist government in Cuba, many Cubans have come to the United States to enjoy freedoms and economic opportunities not available in their own country. At certain times, the U.S. government has welcomed Cuban refugees, but at other times, U.S. government policy has made it difficult for Cubans to enter the country legally. The Cuban government has generally not allowed people to leave Cuba legally. Over the years, many Cubans have left their country secretly, traveling to south Florida on small, tightly packed boats or rafts. Crossing the water to Florida's shores is dangerous, and not all passengers have survived the journey.

This Cuban family in Florida enjoys dining at a Cuban restaurant.

More than one million people from around the world visit Little Havana each year for the Calle Ocho street festival.

In 1980, Castro's government let about 125,000 Cubans leave the country. Many traveled to the Miami area in small boats, some of which were provided by Cuban Americans. This event became known as the Mariel boatlift, because the refugees left from that Cuban port. Since a small number of the refugees had been released from Cuban jails, some Floridians at first did not trust the new arrivals. They worried that they would not know the difference between criminals and law-abiding Cubans. This tension made it more difficult for many of the Cubans to find jobs and acceptance.

Today, the Cuban-American community in Florida is a thriving community of well over one million people that plays a major role in the state's economy, cultural life, and politics. A number of Cuban Americans have been elected to the U.S. Congress. The largest concentration of Cuban Americans is in the Miami area. In fact, a part of Miami is called Little Havana, named after Cuba's capital city. Relations between the United States and Cuba have recently improved somewhat. In 2009, President Barack Obama lifted travel restrictions to Cuba for Cuban Americans. The changes made it easier for Cuban Americans to visit and also to send money to family members who are still living in Cuba.

People from Elsewhere in the Americas

Cubans are far from the only group of immigrants to Florida from the Caribbean and Latin America. As of 2007, the state's population included almost one million people of Mexican or Central American heritage. About 225,000 Floridians were people who came from or whose ancestors came from the Caribbean island of Jamaica. About 372,000 Floridians had come from, or their ancestors had come from, the Caribbean country of Haiti, which is one of the

Many Haitians take great risks to leave their impoverished nation. In 1994, the U.S. Coast Guard intercepted Haitians on an overcrowded boat during a perilous journey to Florida.

poorest countries in the world. In recent decades, many thousands of Haitians have tried to leave the country to find opportunity elsewhere. Many of these people have set out in small, overcrowded boats to reach the coast of south Florida. Some die at sea trying to make the trip.

African Americans in Florida

Florida is home to many African Americans. Some black Floridians have come from other states or countries. Others have lived in Florida for generations.

A community, later known as Overtown, was set up in the northwestern section of Miami in 1896. At that time, laws in the South forced black people and white people to live separately. African Americans who worked in Miami lived in this part of town. Some of them worked in hotels, on the railroads, or in other businesses in Miami. Over the years, their hard work helped develop Miami and surrounding areas. African Americans in Overtown were proud of their community. They had schools, businesses, and churches. In the 1960s, laws outlawing segregation were passed.

In 1960, people picketed in front of Tallahassee stores that refused to serve black people at their lunch counters.

Young beauty queens wave to the crowds at the Florida Strawberry Festival, held each spring in Plant City.

Many people who were living in Overtown chose to leave, but some stayed. Today, efforts are being made to revitalize Overtown and to remind people of its successes and historical importance.

From Near and Far

Floridians come from all different walks of life. A large portion of the population has relocated from other states, including many people who have chosen to retire in Florida. Retirement homes and communities in Florida are very popular. Many retirees come to the state to enjoy the weather and relax. They may be from different ethnic and economic backgrounds. What they have in common is an appreciation for the Sunshine State.

Many people retire to Florida for its warm weather and beaches—and the chance to relax with family.

The Important Issue of Education

Education is an important issue for many Floridians. Florida's education system has seen great improvements since the late 1990s. The high school graduation rate for the 2007–2008 school year was 75 percent—that was a fifteen-point increase over ten years. In addition, reading and math scores have been on the rise. Many attribute Florida's success to the A+ Plan. One part of the plan helps identify schools with underperforming students. These schools get money to improve resources to help students perform at grade level. Another feature of the plan rewards teachers whose students show marked improvements on statewide

Over the past decade, Florida has seen great progress in its education system.

tests. The goal is to make sure that all of Florida's students have the chance to excel. In 2008, the U.S. Department of Education selected Florida to participate in the differentiated accountability pilot project. This program helps the state provide assistance to schools that need it most.

Florida has a vast college and university system. The State University System, which includes eleven schools around the state, educates a total of more than 300,000 students. Florida also has dozens of private colleges and universities, serving more than 120,000 students, as well as a number of community colleges.

Children visit the oldest wooden schoolhouse in the United States. The Saint Augustine building was built in the early 1700s.

Quick Facts

GATORADE
In 1965, a University of Florida football coach wanted to find a way to help his team, the Gators. Players were affected by the heat during games. He spoke to a group of university physicians, who then went into a lab and created a drink to replace the essential components being lost through sweat and exercise. They called the beverage Gatorade.

Calendar of Events

★ Daytona 500

Daytona Beach is famous for this annual February event. Tickets to watch the stock car races are often sold out a year in advance. The races, which originally took place on the beach, are now held at the Daytona International Speedway.

★ Florida State Fair

Agricultural and equestrian events are the focal point of this annual state fair in February. Carnival rides, lots of good food, famous performers, and even clowns attract people to Tampa from all over the state.

★ Swamp Cabbage Festival

During the last full weekend in February, the town of LaBelle hosts this festival, named for the Florida state tree: the sabal, or cabbage, palm. This annual event features a rodeo, a parade, armadillo races, and food made from the sabal palm tree.

★ Silver Spurs Rodeo

In February and in June, crowds flock to Kissimmee to watch rodeo riders compete for big money. Rodeo riders rope cattle and ride bucking broncos for delighted audiences.

★ Weeki Wachee Swamp Fest

In March, this annual festival is held on the banks of the Weeki Wachee River. This family-oriented event includes arts-and-crafts booths, music and dance performances, and a swamp monster costume contest.

★ Springtime Tallahassee

This festival in late March is one of the Southeast's largest. It features great food, a variety of live music, parades, and balloon races.

★ SunFest

From late April to early May, Florida's largest waterfront music and art festival takes place in West Palm Beach.

★ Wausau Funday & Possum Festival

In August, the town of Wausau honors the opossum, known locally as the possum, with activities such as a 5-kilometer race, a parade, and corn-bread baking. There is even possum ice cream and possum stew.

★ Saint Augustine's Birthday Celebration

On the Saturday of Labor Day weekend, the Spanish landing of 1565 is reenacted at the shoreline where the first settlers stepped off their ships.

How the Government Works

The state government of Florida is organized into three branches. The executive branch is headed by the governor. The legislative branch makes the state's laws, and the judicial branch includes the state's courts.

Each town or city in Florida has its own local government, run by a mayor, selectmen, or a council of officials. Voters in the towns and cities elect their local government officials. Each town or city belongs to a county. The counties are made up of several towns or cities. Often, there are governmental positions for the counties.

In 1968, Florida adopted a new state constitution. The legislature can propose changes, or amendments, to this constitution. Three-fifths of each legislative house must approve the proposed amendment. Citizens may also propose amendments by presenting a petition signed by a certain number of voters. For an amendment to be adopted, it must be approved by a majority vote of the people in an election.

The state government of Florida has also created special districts with governmental rights. These districts are not necessarily towns or cities. But it is important for these special districts to have a say in, and some control over, what occurs within them. For example, a special district was approved for Walt Disney World during the 1960s. This allows the Disney company to oversee the drainage of land in its area.

During the American Revolution, Saint Augustine's Castillo de San Marcos served as a base of operations for the British-controlled colony of East Florida.

Branches of Government

EXECUTIVE ★ ★ ★ ★ ★ ★ ★ ★

The governor is the chief executive of the state of Florida. He or she serves a four-year term and cannot serve more than two terms in a row. The governor is responsible for appointing the heads of many state government agencies and for appointing many of the state's judges. The governor also signs or rejects bills that may or may not become laws.

LEGISLATIVE ★ ★ ★ ★ ★ ★ ★ ★

Like most other states and the federal government, Florida's lawmakers are divided into two houses: the senate, with 40 members, and the house of representatives, with 120 members. These legislators represent certain parts of the state. The residents of those districts elect these lawmakers. Senators serve four-year terms and representatives serve two-year terms. Members of the senate or the house of representatives must live in the district they represent and be at least twenty-one years old. They cannot hold office for more than eight years in a row.

JUDICIAL ★ ★ ★ ★ ★ ★ ★ ★

The Florida courts decide whether someone accused of a crime has broken the law as well as settling disputes between individuals or companies. Most cases start in a trial, or circuit, court. Decisions of trial courts can be appealed to one of Florida's five district courts. District court decisions can be appealed to the state's highest court, the Florida supreme court, whose seven justices are appointed to six-year terms by the governor.

How a Bill Becomes a Law

Every year, Florida's house of representatives and senate meet to discuss the issues that are important to the people of the state. In recent years, those issues have included crime, education, the environment, and the economy. Legislators decide whether new laws should be created or old laws changed. Suggestions for new laws can come from the senate or the house of representatives.

These suggestions are called bills. A committee discusses a proposed bill. Members of the committee can make changes to the bill, and the committee rejects or approves it. Once the committee has approved a bill, it goes to the entire house to review. Like the committee, the entire house can change the bill, and it then rejects or approves the bill.

Both houses must approve a bill before it can become a law. A bill passed in one house goes to the other house for review. Once both houses approve the bill, it goes to the governor, who can sign and approve the bill, or reject—or veto—it. If the governor approves the bill, it becomes a law. If the governor vetoes the bill, the state legislature can override the veto with a two-thirds' vote in both houses. If the governor takes no action, the bill becomes a law after sixty days.

What You Can Do

America has a long history of ordinary citizens making extraordinary changes. Although it often seems as if one person cannot make a difference, that is certainly not true. In Florida, the Governor's Points of Light Award is presented every

The twenty-two-story Florida State Capitol stands in Tallahassee.

Contacting Lawmakers

★ ★ ★ ★ ★ ★ ★ ★ ★ ★ ★ ★

Floridians can contact members of the state legislature to make their views known. To get an e-mail or mailing address for a state senator or representative, you can go to this website:

http://www.leg.state.fl.us/kids/whois/ index.html

week to volunteers in the state who are active in their community. Floridians of all ages have won this award.

The Florida legislature has programs to get young people involved in government. The state house of representatives has a page and messenger program, in which each representative sponsors one page (age twelve to fourteen) and one messenger (age fifteen to eighteen) for a week. The state senate has a page program for students fifteen to eighteen years of age. The young people deliver messages, distribute materials, and even sit in on committee meetings.

Every year, almost 250 middle and high school students work in Florida's house of representatives' page and messenger program. These students are part of the 2010 program.

Floridians make a difference by volunteering in many ways, including collecting trash on their beaches as part of an international coastal cleanup.

But you do not need to join a government organization to make a difference in your state. You can help out at homeless centers, animal shelters, or assisted-living communities. You can work for a candidate running for political office or lend a hand at a food kitchen. There are hundreds of volunteer opportunities. You can also make sure you are aware of what is going on around your state. Try to listen to or read your local and state news. There might be issues about which you feel strongly. You can make a difference.

Quick Facts

FLORIDA IN THE U.S. CONGRESS

Florida voters elect people to represent the state in the U.S. Congress. The state has two senators in the U.S. Senate. As of 2010, Florida had twenty-five members in the U.S. House of Representatives.

Making a Living

Floridians earn a living in many different ways. The majority of state residents work in service industries, helping other people or businesses. Service workers in Florida include salesclerks, real estate agents who sell homes or other property, hotel desk clerks, food servers in restaurants, and even the people who wear Mickey Mouse costumes at Disney World. Since Florida is the vacation capital of the world, it is no wonder so many people work in service jobs. But the state's economy—all the goods people make, what they sell, and the services they provide to others—is more than just service jobs. Agriculture, manufacturing, and mining are also important parts of Florida's economy.

Tops in Tourism

Florida's economy relies heavily on tourism. Many Florida businesses depend on the money tourists spend. Many Florida workers provide goods and services to visitors. Also, the state government depends on tourism for a significant portion of the state's tax revenue because Florida has no state income tax. People who live and work in Florida do not have to give part of the money they earn (their income) to the state.

The major way that the state collects money for government programs is through the state sales tax. The sales tax is added to goods and services sold in the state. The state collects this money from the companies that sell the goods

People visit Florida year-round to enjoy water sports such as snorkeling.

Scuba diving in Florida's waters is a popular activity.

and services. Florida residents pay a large part of the sales tax, of course. But if tourists did not come to the state to stay in hotels or campgrounds, eat in restaurants, shop in stores, and more, the state of Florida would collect less money to pay for government services.

The tourist industry brought $65 billion into the economy of Florida in 2008. From July 2007 to June 2008, the state sales tax (paid by both residents and

Workers & Industries

Industry	Number of People Working in That Industry	Percentage of All Workers Who Are Working in That Industry
Education and health care	1,567,280	19%
Wholesale and retail businesses	1,358,423	16%
Publishing, media, entertainment, hotels, and restaurants	1,072,962	13%
Professionals, scientists, and managers	986,276	12%
Construction	839,310	10%
Banking and finance, insurance, and real estate	692,391	8%
Manufacturing	493,522	6%
Other services	435,495	5%
Transportation and public utilities	431,222	5%
Government	410,385	5%
Farming, fishing, forestry, and mining	87,373	1%
Totals	**8,374,639**	**100%**

Notes: Figures above do not include people in the armed forces. "Professionals" includes people such as doctors and lawyers. Percentages may not add to 100 because of rounding.

Source: U.S. Bureau of the Census, 2007 estimates

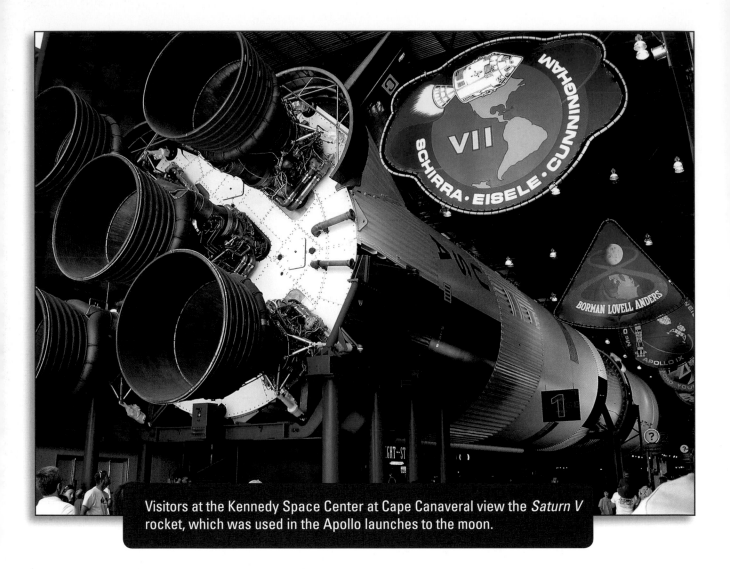

Visitors at the Kennedy Space Center at Cape Canaveral view the *Saturn V* rocket, which was used in the Apollo launches to the moon.

FLAGLER'S FLORIDA

Florida's early development as a tourist destination was largely due to a nineteenth-century oilman named Henry Flagler. Visiting the Sunshine State from his New York City home a few times convinced Flagler that Florida would make a perfect vacation spot. The business tycoon began building hotels and buying railroad lines. As the railway moved south from Jacksonville, Flagler developed places along the route, such as Miami. By 1912, Flagler's Florida East Coast Railway extended all the way to Key West.

tourists) brought in $21.5 billion to pay for government programs. Unfortunately, by the next year, the tourist industry—and the economy as a whole—did not do as well. As a result, the state collected only $19.2 billion in sales taxes. That meant that Florida's state government had less money to repair its roads and bridges, buy school supplies, provide housing to needy residents, and pay for teachers, police officers, and sanitation workers.

In Florida's tourist industry, Disney is tops. Walt Disney World brings money and jobs into the state. Because of Disney's success, other theme parks have been built in the Orlando area. Hotels have sprung up there and elsewhere in the state to give the tourists a place to stay. Cruise ships dock in Florida ports every day, bringing many tourist dollars into the state.

The sale of fresh produce, such as these tomatoes and squash at a Jacksonville farmers market, is an important part of the state's economy.

Throughout the year, tourists take advantage of the state's warm weather and outdoor activities. Florida's beaches are very popular. Some people visit the Everglades to see the state's wildlife. The Florida Keys are also an appealing destination. The islands are ideal for snorkeling, diving, swimming, fishing, exploring the tropical wilderness, visiting historic sites, or enjoying the local events. Many tourists visit the Kennedy Space Center at Cape Canaveral to learn about space exploration.

Products from the Land

Tourism is not the only way people and companies in the state of Florida make money. Livestock is important, although agriculture was the first major industry, and it continues to be important today. Florida is the second-largest agricultural state in the southeast, after North Carolina. It is the eleventh-largest agricultural state in the United States, with sales of agricultural products totaling nearly $7.8 billion a year. Of that total, about $1.4 billion a year comes from sales of vegetables. Florida ranks number two, after California, in vegetable production.

The star of agriculture in Florida, though, is the orange. Florida ranks first among all states in orange juice production. Farmers harvest peanuts and pecans in northern Florida. Cauliflower, broccoli, and sweet corn also grow in Florida.

Seminole Indian ranchers round up their cattle.

RECIPE FOR FLORIDA KEY LIME PIE

This dessert makes use of one of Florida's citrus treasures—the Key lime. Tart and sweet at the same time, this pie is a perfect treat for a hot summer day. Be sure to ask an adult for permission before you begin baking.

WHAT YOU NEED

Filling:

Two 8-ounce packages (a total of 450 grams) cream cheese

Two 14-ounce cans (a total of 750 g) sweetened condensed milk

$^3/_4$ cup (177 milliliters) Key lime juice

1 teaspoon (5 ml) freshly grated lime rind (zest)

$^1/_4$ teaspoon (1.5 g) salt

Topping:

1 cup (237 ml) chilled heavy cream

1 teaspoon (5 ml) vanilla extract

3 tablespoons (24 g) confectioners' sugar

Crust:

One 9-inch (23-cm) graham cracker crust

Before you begin, take the cream cheese out of the refrigerator and let it soften. Then whip the cream cheese in a large bowl until it is fluffy. Add the condensed milk, Key lime juice, lime rind, and salt. Continue to whip the mixture until it is smooth. Pour the filling into the crust. Cover it with plastic wrap and place it in the refrigerator until completely chilled.

To make the topping for your pie, whip the chilled cream in a separate bowl with beaters until it is fluffy. Add the vanilla and confectioners' sugar. Whip the mixture just a little bit more until the ingredients are well blended. Cover the topping with plastic wrap and let the mixture chill in the refrigerator for at least two hours. When you are ready to serve your pie, take out the crust and filling, add the topping, spread it evenly over the pie, and enjoy.

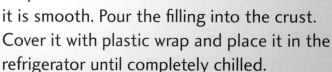

In February and March, boxcars filled with winter produce head north out of Florida. This produce includes snap beans, squash, celery, and tomatoes. These foods ship mostly to states where the winters are cold and the growing seasons are short.

Florida leads the nation in the sale of many major fruits and vegetables. Among other types of fruit, Florida farms grow oranges, grapefruits, mangoes, watermelons, tangerines, limes, and tangelos. Farmers also grow vegetables such as peppers, sweet corn, cucumbers, and beans. Because of year-round warm weather, the state also provides the rest of the country with houseplants, ferns, and flowers.

Ranches around the state breed cattle for the beef industry. Cows are raised on dairy farms, as well. Ranchers also raise hogs and poultry.

Florida is one of the leading suppliers of phosphate. Phosphate is mined in Florida and shipped to the rest of the country and around the world. Most phosphate is used to make plant fertilizers. Other products in which phosphate is used include food for farm animals.

Making Things

There are factories across Florida, although manufacturing plays a small role in the state's economy. At food processing plants, many of the state's agricultural products, such as citrus fruits, are made into juices and jams. Paper mills also dot the state.

Companies in the state make equipment needed to run the space programs at Cape Canaveral. The state also has military and aerospace industries. New technology is developed at government labs. This technology is important for both space exploration and military defense.

Quick Facts

AREA CODE 321
In 1999, the part of Florida that includes Cape Canaveral got a new area code: 321. This number was chosen because it is the end of a space-launch countdown (3-2-1 liftoff!).

The space shuttle *Atlantis* lifted off from the Kennedy Space Center on November 16, 2009, for a ten-day mission to deliver supplies to the International Space Station.

Citrus Fruits

Florida produces more than 70 percent of all of the citrus fruits eaten in the United States. The state's warm climate makes it the perfect place for citrus plants. Florida's farmers grow oranges mostly for their juice. Juices from Florida are sold all around the world.

Fishing

The fishing industry in Florida brings in millions of dollars a year. Fishers make the most money from shrimp, lobsters, and scallops. Saltwater fish such as grouper, mackerel, and red snapper are also moneymakers. A popular freshwater fish is catfish.

Lumber

Forests cover nearly half of Florida. They are filled mostly with pine trees. Florida's forests supply materials for nearly five thousand different products, including paper products and wood for houses.

Spectator Sports

People from all over the world flock to Florida for its sporting events. Football, baseball, basketball, and ice hockey games and horse races are popular attractions. Throughout the year, visitors come to the state to see car races.

Theme Parks

Ever since Walt Disney World opened, theme parks have been a key part of the state's tourism industry. The state has water parks, parks based on movie studios, wildlife parks, and amusement parks with games and rides. The popularity of these places keeps people coming to the state year after year.

Sugarcane

Sugarcane is a tall plant that grows well in tropical climates. It has thick stalks that store a sugary liquid that can be purified to make sugar. After extracting the sugar from the canes, sugar mills then use the stalks as fuel to make electricity. Florida is the country's leading producer of sugarcane.

Keeping a Balance

Florida's population and economy have grown tremendously in recent decades. This growth has led to the construction of many homes, businesses, schools, and highways. It has increased demand for such things as water and electricity as well as the amount of waste to be disposed of. These and other changes have put pressure on the state's environment and natural resources. An issue for Floridians today is how to strike the right balance between continuing the state's growth and protecting its environment.

One of Florida's great natural resources is its coral reefs. Florida is the only place in the United States with a long line of coral reefs in its coastal waters. Coral reefs are underwater formations made up of both living and nonliving elements. The base of a coral reef is limestone. Most of this limestone is the skeletons of dead corals (a type of marine animal). Living corals make up the top of the reef, closest to the surface of the water. Coral reefs provide shelter and food for many underwater plants and animals. They also protect the land from waves from the ocean. Many medicines are made from plants and animals living on or among coral reefs.

Every year, thousands of scuba divers and snorkelers—both tourists and state residents—visit Florida's coral reefs. Some

After burying her freshly laid eggs in the sand, this endangered leatherback turtle crawls back into the sea.

A two-person submarine called the *Super Aviator* explores the fragile coral reefs off the Florida Keys.

touch or step on the living corals. Broken or scraped corals can become infected and die. Boaters and fishers also accidentally start these infections when they hit the corals. Corals also need clear, clean water to grow. Water pollution from factories, cities, and farms has become a problem in Florida.

The state government and the U.S. Coral Reef Task Force have tried to protect Florida's coral reefs. But they cannot do it alone. It is up to both residents and visitors to understand that in a matter of seconds they can destroy some of the rare beauty of a coral reef.

State Flag & Seal

Florida's flag is white with two bold red stripes that begin at each edge and form a large X. In the middle of the flag is Florida's state seal.

The official seal shows rays of sunshine on the Florida coast. It shows a Seminole woman spreading flowers, a sabal palm, and a steamboat. At the bottom of the seal is the state's motto, "In God We Trust." Some aspects, such as the native dress, the steamboat design, and the tree were incorrectly drawn in the original version from 1868. The state adopted this corrected version in 1985.

Blackwater
River State
Forest
△ Britton Hill
Lake
Seminole

29
90
331
231
10

Pensacola
98
90
San Rosa I.

Panama City
Apalachicola

319
Tallahassee
27
27

Apalachicola
National Forest
St. Marks National
Wildlife Refuge

98

Cape San Blas
St. Vincent National
Wildlife Refuge

St. George
Island

Apalachee
Bay

Lower
Suwanee National
Wildlife Refuge
Horseshoe Point

19

221
129
90
41

Osceola
National
Forest

441
10
Jacksonville

75
301

Gainesville
Ocala
National
Forest
17

Lake
George

St. Johns R.

ATLANTIC
OCEAN

95

1

Timucuan Ecological
& Historic Preserve

98
41

Ocala

Daytona
International
Speedway

95

Daytona Beach
Canaveral
National Seashore
John F. Kennedy
Space Center

Cape Canaveral

19

Chassahowitzka
National Wildlife
Refuge

Withlacoochee
State Forest

98
301

Titusville
Orlando
Kissimmee

Walt Disney
World Resort

4

27

Melbourne

192

Florida's Turnpike

95

19
75
41

Clearwater
Tampa
St. Petersburg

Tampa
Bay

Sarasota

17

Lake
Kissimmee

Kissimmee R.

98
441

Port St. Lucie

St. Lucie
Canal

1

West Palm Beach

Gulf of
Mexico

Port
Charlotte

41

Charlotte
Harbor

75

Cape Coral
Sanibel I.

Caloosahatchee R.

Fort Myers

OKALOACOOCHEE
SLOUGH

BIG CYPRESS
SWAMP

Big Cypress
National Preserve

Cape Romano

41

Lake
Okeechobee

27

Arthur R. Marshall Loxahatchee
National Wildlife Refuge

27

Coral Springs
Ft. Lauderdale
Hollywood

Hialeah
Miami

Miami Beach

Biscayne Bay

THE EVERGLADES

Everglades
National Park

Ponce de Leon Bay
Cape Sable

Florida
Bay

Key Largo

1

Dry Tortugas
National Park

Dry Tortugas

Key West

Marquessas
Keys

FLORIDA KEYS

miles

0
150

N
W   E
S

Interstate

Major
Highway

Florida's Turnpike

City or Town

State Capital

Highest Point
in State

Historic Site

National Forest

State Forest

National Park

National Wildlife Refuge

State Park

Other Points of Interest

State Song

The Swanee River (Old Folks at Home)

words and music by Stephen Collins Foster

BOOKS

Cannavale, Matthew C. *Voices from Colonial America: Florida 1513–1821*. Washington, D.C.: National Geographic Society, 2006.

Jankowski, Susan. *Everglades National Park: Adventure, Explore, Discover*. Berkeley Heights, NJ: Enslow Publishers, 2008.

Johnson, Russell W., and Annie P. Johnson. *My Florida Facts*. Sarasota, FL: Pineapple Press, 2009.

Lantz, Peggy Sias. *The Young Naturalist's Guide to Florida: 2nd Edition*. Sarasota, FL: Pineapple Press, 2006.

McCarthy, Kevin M. *Suwannee River Guidebook*. Sarasota, FL: Pineapple Press, 2009.

Young, Jeff C. *Hernando de Soto: Spanish Conquistador in the Americas*. Berkeley Heights, NJ: Enslow Publishers, 2009.

WEBSITES

Everglades National Park—For Kids:
http://www.nps.gov/ever/forkids/index.htm

Florida Kids Home Page:
http://dhr.dos.state.fl.us/kids

Florida's Official Website:
http://www.myflorida.com

Kennedy Space Center Attractions:
http://www.kennedyspacecenter.com/attractions.aspx

Debra Hess has created many different types of educational materials for children across America. She was also the editor of *Scholastic Action Magazine*, a publication for at-risk middle and high school students. Hess has been the Creative Director for Children's Content at a research division of AT&T, has written for an award-winning children's television series, and is the author of dozens of books for children.

Lori P. Wiesenfeld has spent most of her career in reference, children's, and educational publishing. She was the managing editor of *The World Almanac and Book of Facts* and *The World Almanac for Kids*. Before that, she was an editor for *Funk & Wagnalls New Encyclopedia*. She is currently a freelance editor, working on a wide variety of publications.

Page numbers in **boldface** are illustrations.